The Story of Flight

The Wright Brothers and Other
PIONEERS of FLIGHT

Crabtree Publishing Company
www.crabtreebooks.com

PMB 16A, 350 Fifth Avenue,
Suite 3308
New York, NY 10118

612 Welland Avenue
St. Catharines, Ontario
L2M 5V6

Published in 2003 by
Crabtree Publishing Company

Coordinating editor: Ellen Rodger
Project editors: Sean Charlebois, Carrie Gleason
Production coordinator: Rose Gowsell

Created and Produced by
David West 🧍🧍 Children's Books

Project Development, Design, and Concept
David West Children's Books:
Designer: Rob Shone
Editor: James Pickering
Illustrators: Gerry Haylock & Neil Reed
(Allied Artists), James Field & Ross Watton (SGA), Gary
Slater & Steve Weston (Specs Art), Rob Perry & Colin
Howard (Advocate)
Picture Research: Carlotta Cooper

Photo Credits:
Abbreviations: t-top, m-middle, b-bottom, r-right,
l-left, c-center.

Front cover tm & pages 13tr, 19bl, 20tl - The Flight
Collection. 4tr (G1 F1), 6tl (GB 7), 7br (FA03611),
8tl (G1 03), 9tr (X002-8057), 10tl (G1 02) & ml
(PC 75/9/N1633), 12tl (PC 76/17/2), 14tl (G1 P3),
16tl (PC 72/225/8) & ml (PC 72/75/116), 18tl
(X002-8006/002/R33), 21tr (X002-8006/002/R39),
22bl (X001-2785/050), 25tr (PC 72/151/18) & bl
(X002-9506/008), 26m (X001-2785/139/004) & br
(X002-9571/001), 29tr - Royal Air Force Museum.
5tr - Dover Books. 14ml - Ole Steen Hansen. 26tl -
Novosti (London). 28tl - Rex Features Ltd.

06 05 04 03
10 9 8 7 6 5 4 3 2 1

Printed and bound in Dubai

Cataloging in Publication Data
Hansen, Ole Steen.
    The Wright brothers and other pioneers of flight / Ole Steen
Hansen.
        p. cm. -- (The story of flight)
Includes index.
ISBN 0-7787-1200-1 (RLB) -- ISBN 0-7787-1216-8 (PB)
    1. Air pilots--Biography--Juvenile literature. 2. Aeronautics--
History--Juvenile literature. 3. Flight--History--Juvenile literature. [1.
Air pilots. 2. Aeronautics--History. 3. Flight--History.] I. Title: Wright
brothers and other pioneers of flight. II. Title. Series.
    TL539.H27 2003
    629.13'092'2--dc21
                                            2002156485
                                            LC

The Story of Flight

The Wright Brothers and Other PIONEERS of FLIGHT

Ole Steen Hansen

Crabtree Publishing Company
www.crabtreebooks.com

CONTENTS

DA VINCI
As early as the 1500s, artist and scientist Leonardo da Vinci sketched designs for flying machines, such as this helicopter. He never tested them by building them.

THE FIRST MEN TO FLY
On November 1, 1783 two brave men from France, Pilatre de Rozier and Marquis d'Arlandes, became the first to fly. They took off from Paris in a hot air balloon designed by the Montgolfier brothers. Flying was possible after all! Despite their success, there were still people who wanted to create flying machines that were heavier than air.

INTRODUCTION

The early pioneers of flight believed that it was possible for man to fly. They were prepared to sacrifice their time, money, and physical safety to test their inventions. They ignored the laughter of others who thought their experiments were ridiculous, dangerous, unnecessary, and impossible! A few brave souls around the world shared this passion, and eventually they invented the airplane.

EARLY ATTEMPTS
This design for a pedal-powered flying machine dates from 1885. Like many other ideas of the time, this one did not work. Inventing the airplane was not an easy task.

CAYLEY

Many early attempts to fly were based on the idea of bird-like, flapping wings. Inventor and scientist Sir George Cayley realized that an airplane's wings would never be able to provide both lift and thrust, as they do for birds. Fixed wings would have to be used to lift aircraft up into the air. Some sort of engine would then create thrust, which would propel the aircraft forward.

SIR GEORGE CAYLEY
Sir George Cayley's ideas earned him the name "the father of aerial navigation."

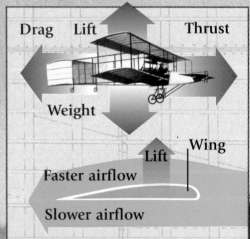

Drag   Lift   Thrust

Weight

Wing

Lift

Faster airflow

Slower airflow

HOW PLANES FLY
Four forces are at work in flight: lift, weight, thrust, and drag. When lift equals weight and thrust equals drag, the aircraft will fly at a steady speed and stay at the same altitude, or height. Lift is created because the air passing over the wing moves at a higher speed. This creates a **low pressure** area which sucks the airplane up into the sky.

Cayley drew designs for **monoplanes**, **biplanes**, and **triplanes**. He built flying models and was the first to think about **streamlining** airplanes to minimize drag. He suggested the use of a **rudder** and **elevators** to control airplanes. All this influenced the thinking of later aircraft designers. Cayley designed two full-size triplane gliders. In 1849, the first glider floated off the ground at the end of a rope, with a ten-year-old boy on board. In the second glider, Cayley sent one of his drivers gliding across a small valley near his home in Yorkshire, England, in 1853. This was the first manned gliding flight in history.

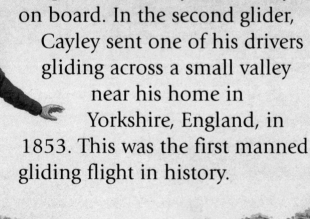

AIRBORNE
Cayley's driver was not happy about his short historic flight and shouted after landing, "I was hired to drive, not to fly!"

The *Aerial Steam Carriage*

Fantastic drawings of the *Aerial Steam Carriage* were published in 1843, but the aircraft could not be built because an engine light and powerful enough for it to fly did not exist. The *Aerial Steam Carriage* had many features that appeared in later aircraft such as light, wire-braced wings, propellers, and an undercarriage. The aircraft itself was never built.

ADER

CLÉMENT ADER
Clément Ader built the first machine to lift off under its own power.

Clément Ader became interested in flying in the 1870s. By 1890, his plane, the *Éole*, was ready to be tested. The wings of the *Éole* looked like the wings of a bat. It was powered by a 20 horsepower (hp) steam engine, also designed by Ader. On October 9, 1890 the *Éole* took off and flew for about 164 feet (50 m). This was the first time in history a machine heavier than air had lifted off from level ground, not down a ramp, and under its own power.

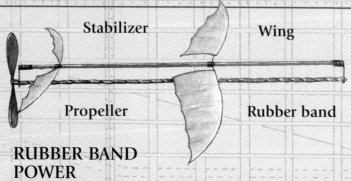

Stabilizer · Wing · Propeller · Rubber band

RUBBER BAND POWER

The French inventor Alphonse Pénaud flew this rubber band-powered model airplane in 1871. It had a wingspan, or length from wingtip to wingtip, of only 18 inches (45 cm) but was stable. If it started to **bank** with one wing higher than the other, it would automatically return to level flight. This was because the wingtips were bent slightly upward. The **tail plane** balanced the nose so it would not move up or down. Future European aviators adopted these ideas and tried to make their airplanes automatically stable in the air, instead of trying to control the planes in flight.

The *Éole* was not a practical airplane.
The steam engine was well designed, but not powerful enough to keep the *Éole* flying. The *Éole* was doomed to crash after a few moments in the air, because it had no controls and no tail to balance it. The bat-like wings could be warped a little for adjustments in the air, but the *Éole* had no other controls for the pilot to use. Like most early European pioneers, Ader thought more about getting airborne than about the problems of controlling an airplane in flight. Ader built two more airplanes, but neither of them could fly.

Maxim's Monster

Sir Hiram Maxim was an American living in England. In 1894 he built a monster biplane that thundered down tracks, driven by two 180 hp steam engines. It had a three-person crew, a wingspan of 104 feet (32 m), which was the same as a four-engined bomber of World War II, and a weight of about 3.5 tons (3,600 kg). The biplane reached a speed of 26 miles per hour (67 km/h), and lifted off, but crashed immediately. Like Ader, Maxim was trying to produce enough power and lift from the wings to get airborne, but could not control his airplane in the air.

THE FIRST HOP

Ader made his powered hop-flight on the grounds of a château near Paris, France. His *Éole* reached an altitude of about 8 inches (20 cm). His seat was behind the boiler, so he could not even see where he was going!

LILIENTHAL

OTTO LILIENTHAL

Otto Lilienthal was an inspiration to the Wright brothers and other pioneers. Photography was a new art at the time and published photos of Lilienthal helped to make his experiments known around the world. Not only was Lilienthal the first person to be photographed in flight, he was also the first to fly in machines that were heavier than air.

Otto Lilienthal was born in Germany in 1848 and was interested in human flight from an early age. Lilienthal built several working gliders and made about 2,500 flights between 1889 and the crash that killed him in 1896.

The experiments of people like Ader and Maxim showed that it was only a matter of time before powered flight would be possible.

Octave Chanute

The French-born American, Octave Chanute, attempted to publish all available information on Lilienthal's and other pioneers' experiments in flight. He designed gliders too, but his writing had the greater impact on the development of aviation. Chanute became a close friend of the Wright brothers and encouraged them to experiment with biplanes rather than monoplanes.

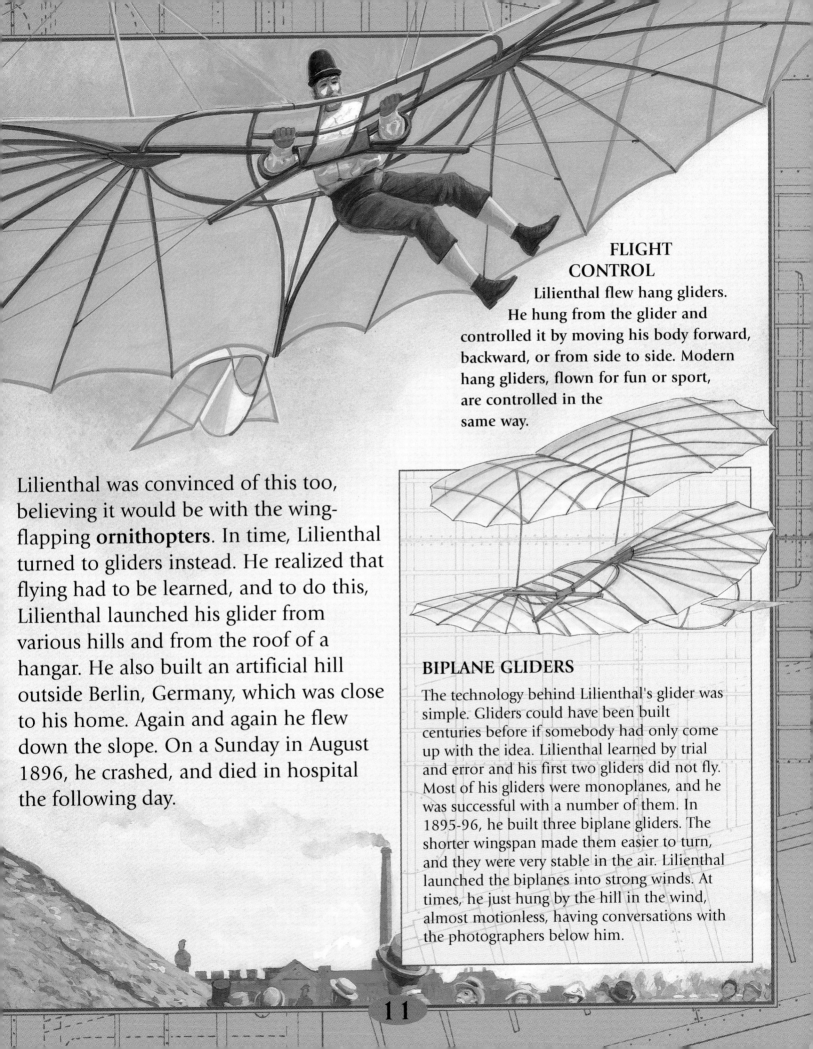

Lilienthal flew hang gliders. He hung from the glider and controlled it by moving his body forward, backward, or from side to side. Modern hang gliders, flown for fun or sport, are controlled in the same way.

Lilienthal was convinced of this too, believing it would be with the wing-flapping **ornithopters**. In time, Lilienthal turned to gliders instead. He realized that flying had to be learned, and to do this, Lilienthal launched his glider from various hills and from the roof of a hangar. He also built an artificial hill outside Berlin, Germany, which was close to his home. Again and again he flew down the slope. On a Sunday in August 1896, he crashed, and died in hospital the following day.

BIPLANE GLIDERS

The technology behind Lilienthal's glider was simple. Gliders could have been built centuries before if somebody had only come up with the idea. Lilienthal learned by trial and error and his first two gliders did not fly. Most of his gliders were monoplanes, and he was successful with a number of them. In 1895-96, he built three biplane gliders. The shorter wingspan made them easier to turn, and they were very stable in the air. Lilienthal launched the biplanes into strong winds. At times, he just hung by the hill in the wind, almost motionless, having conversations with the photographers below him.

Langley

American astronomer S.P. Langley flew six model aircraft like this over distances up to 3,000 feet (900 m). The full-sized planes broke up in 1903 during a launch from a houseboat on the Potomac River in the United States. Newspapers mocked "Langley's Folly" and wrote that flight was impossible, even though the Wrights were actually flying at almost the same time!

FIRST FLIGHT

Orville Wright was the pilot on the world's first powered flight. The brothers had tossed a coin to decide who would fly the plane. His brother Wilbur, who was four years older, flew the longest distance that day.

THE WRIGHT BROTHERS

The Wright brothers were inspired by Lilienthal and agreed with his view that flying had to be learned in the air. They experimented with gliders as well, but soon decided that controls were better than swinging the body as Lilienthal had done.

THE WRIGHT BROTHERS
Orville and Wilbur Wright succeeded where others failed because they studied flight controls. The same basic principles, discovered and described by the Wright brothers, are still used today.

The brothers owned a bicycle business which provided them with money for their experiments. After hundreds of short gliding flights between 1900 and 1902, they developed the controls necessary to fly. They used rudder, elevator, and wing warping to control the plane (later pioneers used **ailerons** to bank the wings). On December 17, 1903, they flew the world's first powered airplane at Kill Devil Hills near Kitty Hawk, North Carolina. The wind was strong and gusty and they flew very low because they had problems controlling the wildly unstable machine. On one flight their *Flyer* touched the ground, but rose again and flew on. The longest flight of the day lasted 59 seconds. The Wright brothers had done what no one had done before. They had invented a powered airplane that could be flown and controlled in the air.

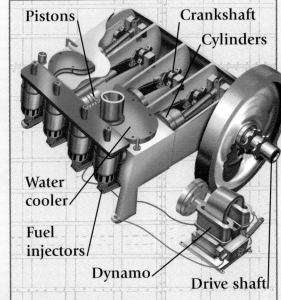

Pistons · Crankshaft · Cylinders · Water cooler · Fuel injectors · Dynamo · Drive shaft

POWER SOURCE
The Wright brothers developed their own engine for the *Flyer*. They had hoped to use a car engine, but discovered they were too heavy compared to the amount of power they provided. The talented brothers then designed and built their own engine!

SANTOS-DUMONT

The first European flights were in 1906. Danish inventor Jacob Ellehammer made a short tethered flight on September 12. Brazilian aviator Alberto Santos-Dumont, living in Paris, made a short flight the next day. These flights were great achievements, but not as spectacular as the flights by the Wright brothers in the United States.

AROUND THE TOWER

In 1901, Santos-Dumont circled the Eiffel Tower in an airship, and landed back at the French *Aéro-Club* outside Paris.

Ellehammer

Like many aviators, Ellehammer was made fun of when he first started to design airplanes. "Prices are going up, everything is going up – except Ellehammer" was a popular joke in Copenhagen, Denmark. He never managed to build a practical airplane, but in 1908 he won a prize at a German airshow by performing a flight that lasted eleven seconds. His aircraft was the only one to take off at all.

SANTOS-DUMONT 14-BIS

Length: 31 ft 10 in (9.7 m)

Wingspan: 36 ft 9 in (11.2 m)

Speed: 25 mph (40 km/h)

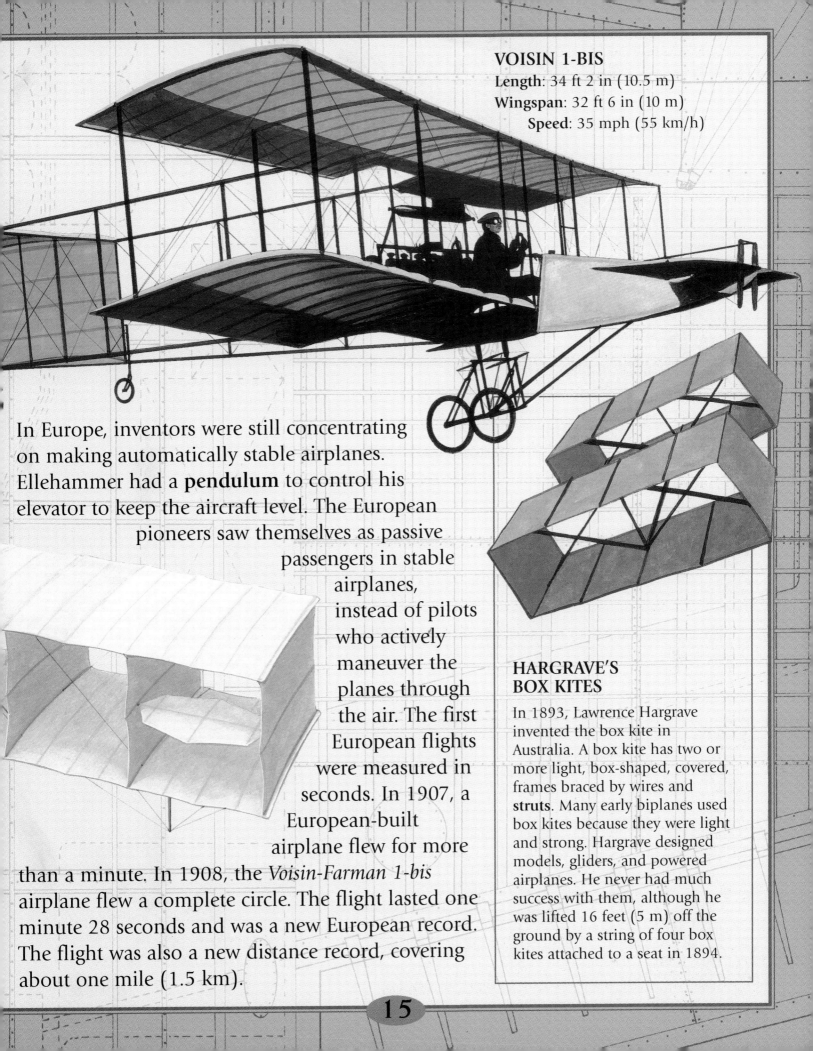

VOISIN 1-BIS
Length: 34 ft 2 in (10.5 m)
Wingspan: 32 ft 6 in (10 m)
Speed: 35 mph (55 km/h)

In Europe, inventors were still concentrating on making automatically stable airplanes. Ellehammer had a **pendulum** to control his elevator to keep the aircraft level. The European pioneers saw themselves as passive passengers in stable airplanes, instead of pilots who actively maneuver the planes through the air. The first European flights were measured in seconds. In 1907, a European-built airplane flew for more than a minute. In 1908, the *Voisin-Farman 1-bis* airplane flew a complete circle. The flight lasted one minute 28 seconds and was a new European record. The flight was also a new distance record, covering about one mile (1.5 km).

HARGRAVE'S BOX KITES

In 1893, Lawrence Hargrave invented the box kite in Australia. A box kite has two or more light, box-shaped, covered, frames braced by wires and **struts**. Many early biplanes used box kites because they were light and strong. Hargrave designed models, gliders, and powered airplanes. He never had much success with them, although he was lifted 16 feet (5 m) off the ground by a string of four box kites attached to a seat in 1894.

15

THE WRIGHT FLYERS

From October 1905 to May 1908, the Wright brothers did not fly. They tried to sell their airplane to the American and British governments, but neither was interested. In 1908, Wilbur went to France to demonstrate the Wright airplane.

PASSENGERS

During 1908, about 60 passengers were carried, one at a time, on Wilbur's flights in Europe.

Town To Town

In France in October 1908, Henry Farman flew from Bouy to Reims. The 16 miles (27 km) were flown in 20 minutes at an altitude of 164 feet (50 m). Farman managed to avoid the windmills and church steeples on his way. For the first time in the history of aviation, two towns had been linked by air.

The elite of European pilots were present when Wilbur took off. "We are as children compared with the Wrights!" and "We are beaten!" were some of the comments from the people watching Wilbur effortlessly bank and turn his aircraft over a racecourse in Le Mans. Because their airplanes were difficult to turn, the Europeans had trouble taking off and landing in the same place. Wilbur flew more than a hundred flights in Europe in 1908. On the last day of the year he was airborne for two hours and 20 minutes. The Europeans were quick to realize how the Wright flight controls worked. They also decided that the Wright *Flyer* could be improved. One improvement was wheels instead of skids, so the plane did not have to take off from a specially prepared track. Wright *Flyers* were also unstable. European builders wanted to make planes that were easy to steer and were also stable.

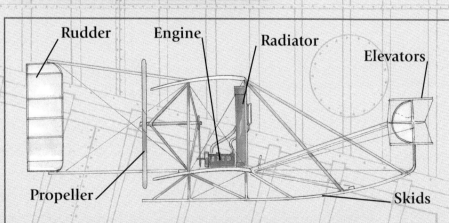

Rudder   Engine   Radiator   Elevators

Propeller   Skids

THE WRIGHT *FLYER III*

The Wrights flew their *Flyer II* in 1904, but the *Flyer III* was the world's first practical airplane. With this, they perfected their system of flight controls. In 1905, they flew the *Flyer III* on many flights. On one occasion they were airborne for 38 minutes and flew a distance of 23 miles (38 km).

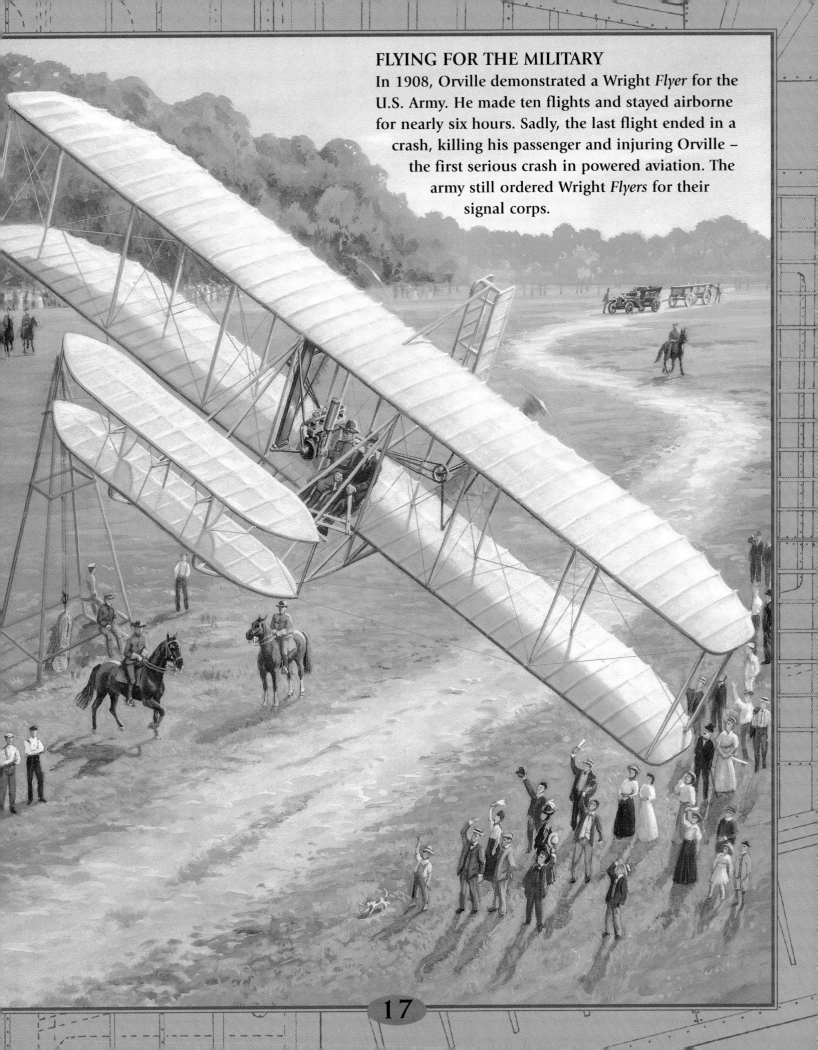

FLYING FOR THE MILITARY

In 1908, Orville demonstrated a Wright *Flyer* for the U.S. Army. He made ten flights and stayed airborne for nearly six hours. Sadly, the last flight ended in a crash, killing his passenger and injuring Orville – the first serious crash in powered aviation. The army still ordered Wright *Flyers* for their signal corps.

BLÉRIOT

BLÉRIOT AND FARMAN
Louis Blériot (right) and Henry Farman (left) were two of the great pioneers of European aviation.

In 1907, the French aviation pioneer Blériot described how easy it was to survive an airplane crash. He had far more experience with crashing than with flying. In 1909, he crossed the English Channel, the body of water that separates Britain and France, with his *Blériot XI*.

The Daily Mail newspaper offered a prize of £1,000, or about $1,550 U.S., to the first pilot to cross the Channel. The British pilot Hubert Latham tried first but ditched his plane *Antoinette* about 7.5 miles (12 km) from the British coast on July 19. Blériot took off from France in the early morning calm six days later.

AIRCRAFT PRODUCER
The success of the Channel flight made Blériot's company the world's largest producer of aircraft between 1909 and 1914. About 900 *Blériot XIs* in different versions were sold to military and civilian customers. Buyers learned to fly for free at Blériot's flying school, though they had to pay for damage to the training plane, adding a lot to the bill!

THE *ANTOINETTE*

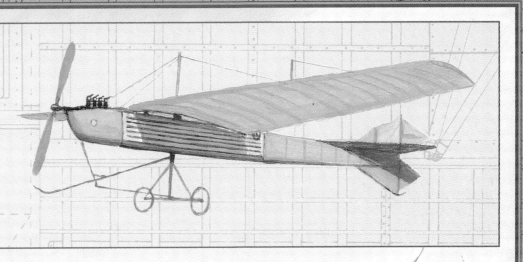

Latham's attempts at flying the English Channel were made with an *Antoinette*. It was a slim-lined airplane and faster than the *Blériot XI*, but Latham's engine failed on both attempts. After ditching the plane in the Channel, he sat on it and waited to be picked up by a ship.

The flight lasted 37 minutes. Blériot drifted slightly in the wrong direction in the fog halfway across the Channel, but soon the British coast appeared. He landed near Dover Castle, where he was greeted by a French journalist waving the French flag. It was the longest crossing of water at the time, and the first time two countries were linked by air. A newspaper claimed: "Great Britain is no longer an island."

Harriet Quimby

In 1912, American journalist Harriet Quimby became the first woman to fly an airplane across the English Channel, in a *Blériot*. Hardly anybody noticed her achievement because the newspapers were focused on the sinking of the Titanic the night before. Quimby died a few months later when she and a passenger were thrown out of her aircraft that suddenly nose-dived. Neither of them wore seatbelts.

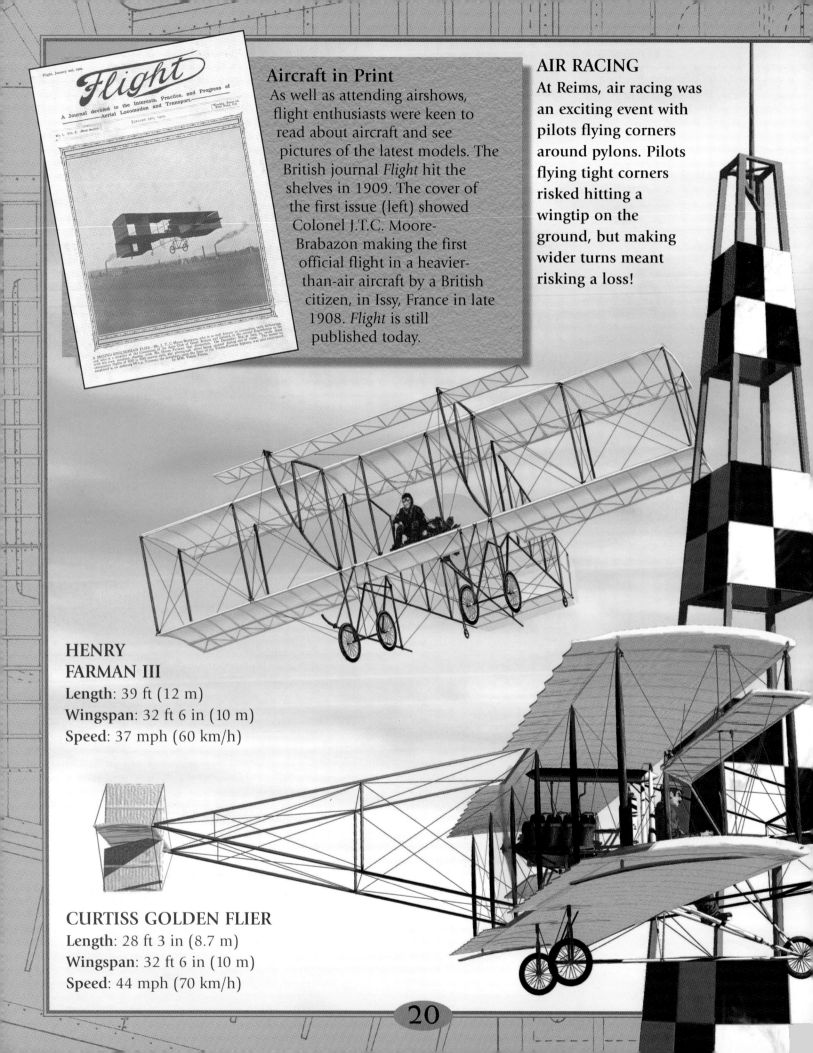

Aircraft in Print

As well as attending airshows, flight enthusiasts were keen to read about aircraft and see pictures of the latest models. The British journal *Flight* hit the shelves in 1909. The cover of the first issue (left) showed Colonel J.T.C. Moore-Brabazon making the first official flight in a heavier-than-air aircraft by a British citizen, in Issy, France in late 1908. *Flight* is still published today.

AIR RACING

At Reims, air racing was an exciting event with pilots flying corners around pylons. Pilots flying tight corners risked hitting a wingtip on the ground, but making wider turns meant risking a loss!

HENRY FARMAN III

Length: 39 ft (12 m)
Wingspan: 32 ft 6 in (10 m)
Speed: 37 mph (60 km/h)

CURTISS GOLDEN FLIER

Length: 28 ft 3 in (8.7 m)
Wingspan: 32 ft 6 in (10 m)
Speed: 44 mph (70 km/h)

THE FIRST AIRSHOWS

The pioneers became heroes as flying grew more popular. Louis Blériot became an international celebrity after his Channel flight. When the world's aviators gathered for the first international aviation meeting at Reims, France in 1909, half a million spectators turned up.

At Reims, Hubert Latham set a new altitude record when he flew to 508 feet (155 m). Henry Farman flew 112 miles (180 km) in 3 hours 5 minutes, and landed almost in darkness – another record. The Gordon Bennett trophy race was won by American pilot Glenn Curtiss. Curtiss beat Blériot by 5.8 seconds. Curtiss had flown at an average speed of 46 miles per hour (74.6 km/h). In 1907, he had set a speed record for motorbikes, driving at 136 miles per hour (219 km/h) – much faster than his airplane speed.

GLENN CURTISS

Glenn Curtiss was one of the greatest American aviation pioneers. He produced the world's first practical seaplanes. Aircraft and engines from his companies flew in both World Wars.

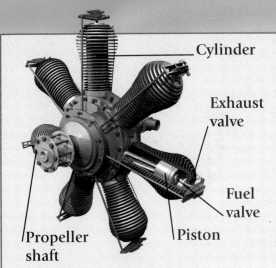

Cylinder

Exhaust valve

Fuel valve

Propeller shaft

Piston

THE ROTARY ENGINE

At the Reims meeting, a rotary engine was demonstrated for the first time. On a rotary engine, the **crankshaft** is attached to the plane. The rest of the engine rotates with the propeller. The rotary engine was very powerful for its weight and much more reliable than other early engines. Rotary engines were used until the end of World War I.

BLÉRIOT XII
Length: 27 ft 6 in (8.5 m)
Wingspan: 30 ft 10 in (9.5 m)
Speed: 48 mph (77 km/h)

RODGERS

In 1911, C.P. Rodgers learned to fly at the flying school set up by the Wright brothers. He flew solo after only 90 minutes of dual instruction. By comparison, today's pilots receive from 10 to 20 hours instruction before they solo. On September 17, 1911, after only 60 hours flying, Rodgers confidently set out to fly across the U.S.

Rodgers was followed by a three-car train carrying his mother, wife, mechanics, spare parts, and fuel. The train bore the name *Vin Fiz*, as did his Wright EX biplane. The company producing the grape-flavored *Vin Fiz* soft drink sponsored him with $5 per mile. The money was much needed as Rodgers repeatedly crashed. On the second day he crashed into a chicken shed and it took three days to repair the plane. He crashed at least 15 more times on the flight.

CALBRAITH PERRY RODGERS

Calbraith Perry Rodgers was a football hero who raced yachts and cars before turning to airplanes. He died in 1912 when he flew into a flock of seagulls. One jammed his rudder and he crashed, breaking his neck and back.

CLAUDE GRAHAM WHITE
LANDING AT WHITE HOUSE, WASHINGTON
TO CALL ON PRESIDENT TAFT
OCTOBER 14, 1910

First Flight to Washington

In 1910, after an aviation meeting, English aviation pioneer Claude Grahame-White became the first pilot to land in the street of a big city when he touched down near the White House in Washington D.C. Sadly, the president was not at home to greet him, but the landing still made the headlines.

GROUND SUPPORT

One of the train cars was fitted out as a repair shop.

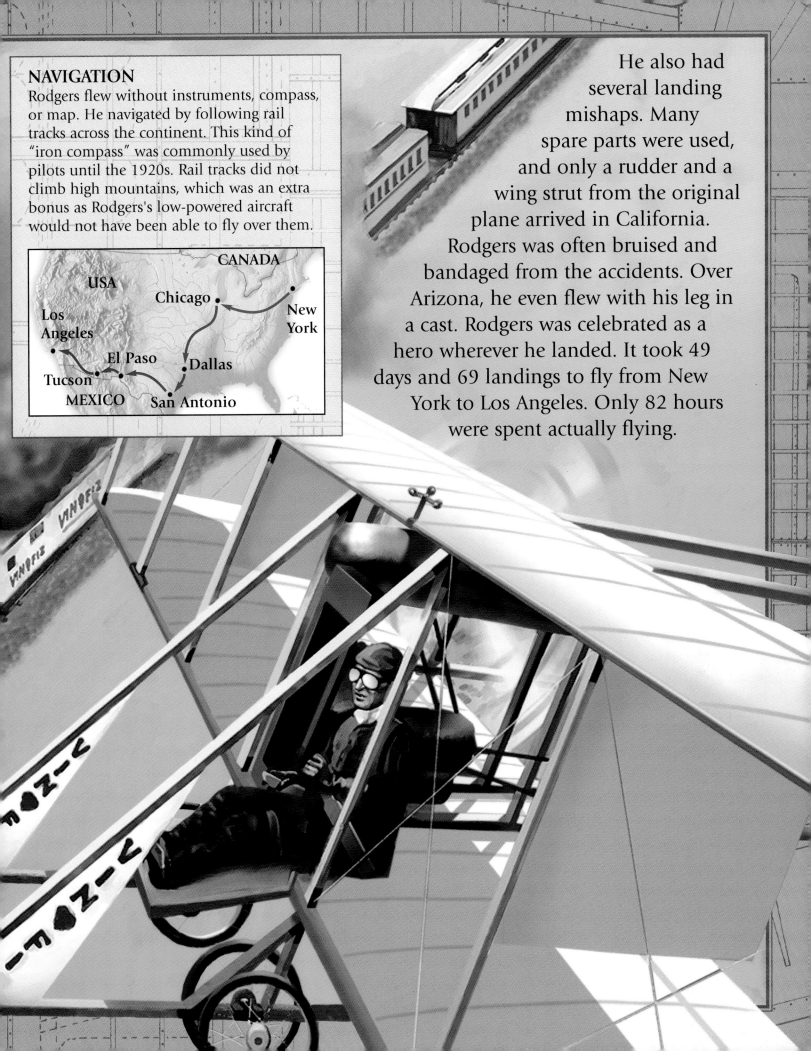

NAVIGATION

Rodgers flew without instruments, compass, or map. He navigated by following rail tracks across the continent. This kind of "iron compass" was commonly used by pilots until the 1920s. Rail tracks did not climb high mountains, which was an extra bonus as Rodgers's low-powered aircraft would not have been able to fly over them.

CANADA

USA

Chicago

New York

Los Angeles

El Paso

Dallas

Tucson

San Antonio

MEXICO

He also had several landing mishaps. Many spare parts were used, and only a rudder and a wing strut from the original plane arrived in California. Rodgers was often bruised and bandaged from the accidents. Over Arizona, he even flew with his leg in a cast. Rodgers was celebrated as a hero wherever he landed. It took 49 days and 69 landings to fly from New York to Los Angeles. Only 82 hours were spent actually flying.

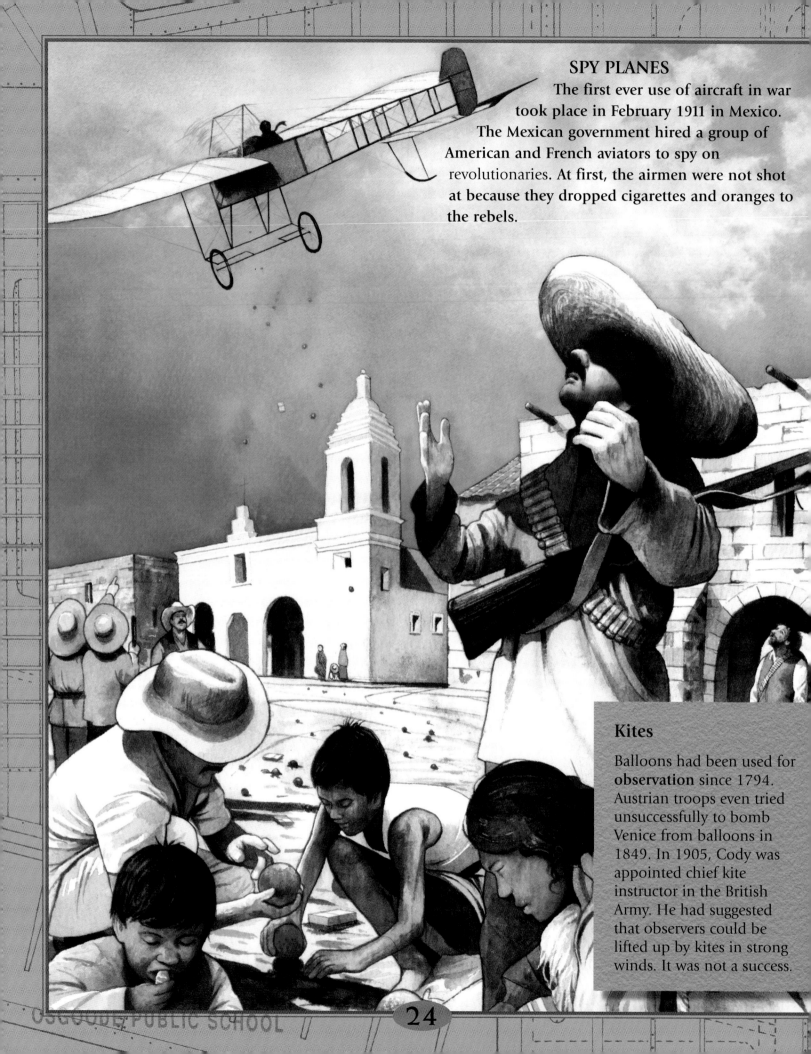

SPY PLANES

The first ever use of aircraft in war took place in February 1911 in Mexico. The Mexican government hired a group of American and French aviators to spy on revolutionaries. At first, the airmen were not shot at because they dropped cigarettes and oranges to the rebels.

Kites

Balloons had been used for **observation** since 1794. Austrian troops even tried unsuccessfully to bomb Venice from balloons in 1849. In 1905, Cody was appointed chief kite instructor in the British Army. He had suggested that observers could be lifted up by kites in strong winds. It was not a success.

MILITARY AIRCRAFT

Could aircraft be used for military purposes? In the early days of flying, many pioneer pilots thought yes. From an aircraft, a pilot would be able to spy on the enemy. At the time it was the job of the cavalry to do this. When aircraft became capable of lifting heavier loads they could drop bombs too.

Many army officers claimed that airplanes would never serve a military purpose. Against much opposition, airplanes were used for observation during British army maneuvers in 1910. Three young officers asked if they could take part with their own aircraft. The results surprised the senior officers, who realized that pilots high in the sky could observe enemy movements far better than cavalry on the ground. Soon after, all bigger nations started to build air squadrons.

S.F. CODY

Texas showman Samuel Franklin Cody experimented with kites and airships. In 1908, he became the first man in Britain to fly when his British Army Airplane No. 1 flew about 1,312 feet (400 m) before it crashed. Cody designed and flew more aircraft but was killed in 1913 when one of his planes broke up in mid-air.

THE FIRST BOMBERS

In 1911, Italian pilots became the first to drop bombs from a plane. They were attacking Turkish positions in Libya, North Africa. The international Hague Convention from 1899 had forbidden the dropping of bombs from balloons. The Italians argued that the rule did not apply to bombs dropped from airplanes!

DAREDEVILS

During the pioneer years pilots and designers learned by trial and error. How strong did an airplane need to be? How did it behave at very slow or very high speeds? In spite of the risks, some pilots took their airplanes to new extremes to explore their potential.

NESTEROV

Petr Nesterov flew his first loop only when he was confident of success. He said he did not want to risk his life "because I'm a father of two children."

In 1913, the Russian military aviator Petr Nesterov performed the first loop ever. He was arrested as soon as he landed for "undue risk with a machine, the property of his government." He was soon released because it was realized that he had a point. In future wars there was going to be fighting in the air, and pilots would have to perform such maneuvers. In western Europe, the first loop was performed by French daredevil aviator Celestin-Adolphe Pégoud.

Aerial Photography

French pilot Pierre Verrier took a cameraperson up in his plane when the pilot Celestin-Adolphe Pégoud looped three times in succession over the gasping crowds at an airfield south of London. The cameraperson filmed Pégoud's loops from the other plane. Verrier was also a pioneer of the dangerous practice of night flying.

Pégoud had already flown an aircraft upside down, even though experts told him it was not possible. Pégoud soon performed his feats in many countries and "looping the loop" became the latest craze at airshows before the First World War. Pégoud was killed in aerial combat in 1915.

BAILING OUT

Pégoud got the inspiration to do the loop when he jumped from his single seat *Blériot* to demonstrate a parachute. When the pilotless aircraft performed strange maneuvers on its way down, he decided that he would also be able to do that if he stayed in the airplane!

LOOPING THE LOOP

The loop is actually an easy maneuver to perform, if your plane has enough speed and its wings are strong enough for it. Old aircraft have to dive to get the speed before looping. The pilot then pulls back the stick and the nose of the aircraft goes up.

SIKORSKY

SIKORSKY
Sikorsky started as a Russian aviation pioneer, but later created helicopters in the United States.

Igor Sikorsky was one of the most talented early pioneers of aviation. He was the son of a doctor in Kiev, Ukraine. Fascinated by accounts of flying, Sikorsky visited Louis Blériot in France to learn about flying. Sikorsky's sister Olga gave him money to build a helicopter in 1909. It was not a success, but like other true pioneers, Sikorsky was not deterred by the failure.

Sikorsky's first plane did not fly, and the next one only flew for eight minutes before crashing. Sikorsky had not flown before, and had no instructor.

HELICOPTER NO1
Sikorsky's first helicopter would not fly and he soon turned to making airplanes. After the **Russian Revolution** and his immigration to the U.S., he designed the world's first successful single rotor helicopter in 1939. Today, Sikorsky helicopters are flying all over the world.

FLYING IN STYLE
In 1914, Sikorsky flew eight passengers on a 2.5-hour sightseeing trip over St. Petersburg, Russia.

Sikorsky learned from his mistakes and went on to design both land and seaplanes. By 1911, he was earning money flying his own designs. Beginning in 1912, Sikorsky designed a series of four-engined biplanes, which were the largest and most efficient airplanes built for transporting goods and people before World War I. They had an enclosed cabin for passengers, a bedroom, a toilet, and an observation platform out front. Mechanics could walk out between the wings and change spark plugs in flight. When World War I broke out, Sikorsky's designs were mostly used for bombers, and not airliners.

CORNU

Paul Cornu was French, and like the Wright brothers, a bicycle maker. In 1907, he built the first helicopter to lift a person. The flight lasted 20 seconds and was flown at an altitude of 12 inches (30 cm). The helicopter had no controls and like Sikorsky's early helicopters it was not developed further.

SPOTTERS' GUIDE

Nearly all early airplanes were based on a wooden frame covered in fabric. This was a good way to produce light, yet strong, air frames, because their engines were not very powerful. The struts and wires caused great air resistance, but because early aircraft flew at very low speed, this was not important.

CAYLEY TRIPLANE GLIDER
Length: 15 ft (4.5 m)
Wingspan: 18 ft (5.5 m)

WRIGHT FLYER
Length: 21 ft (6.5 m)
Wingspan: 40 ft 6 in (12.5 m)
Speed: 30 mph (48 km/h)

LILIENTHAL GLIDER
Length: 15 ft (4.5 m)
Wingspan: 20 ft (6 m)

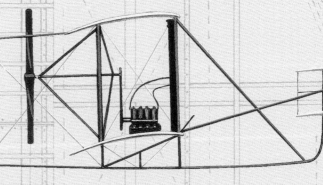

ÉOLE
Length: 16 ft 6 in (5 m)
Wingspan: 46 ft (14 m)

BLÉRIOT XI
Length: 26 ft 3 in (8 m)
Wingspan: 25 ft 6 in (7.8 m)
Speed: 47 mph (75 km/h)

ILYA MOUROMETZ
Length: 66 ft 6 in (20.5 m)
Wingspan: 112 ft 3 in (34.5 m)
Speed: 65 mph (105 km/h)

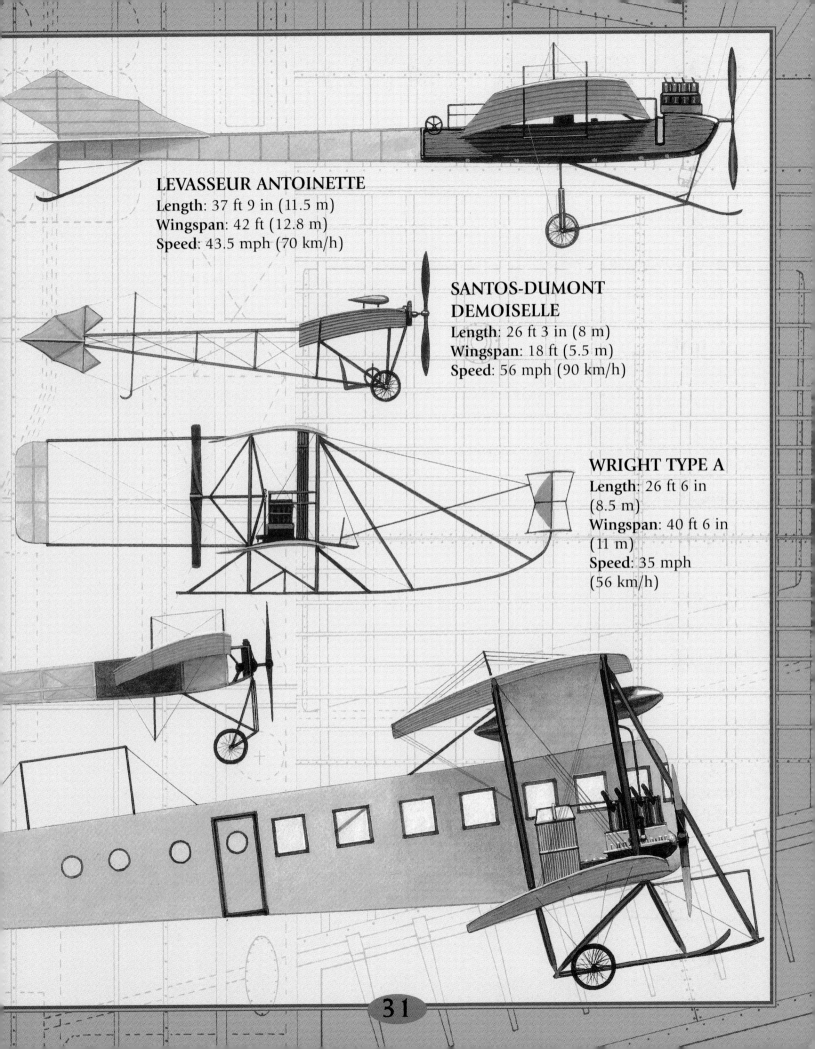

LEVASSEUR ANTOINETTE
Length: 37 ft 9 in (11.5 m)
Wingspan: 42 ft (12.8 m)
Speed: 43.5 mph (70 km/h)

SANTOS-DUMONT DEMOISELLE
Length: 26 ft 3 in (8 m)
Wingspan: 18 ft (5.5 m)
Speed: 56 mph (90 km/h)

WRIGHT TYPE A
Length: 26 ft 6 in (8.5 m)
Wingspan: 40 ft 6 in (11 m)
Speed: 35 mph (56 km/h)

INDEX

GLOSSARY

AILERONS Flaps on the wings that control rolling or banking.

AIRSHIP An aircraft filled with a lighter than air gas that is self-propelled.

BANK The tilt of the aircraft to one side during a turn.

BIPLANE An aircraft that has two sets of wings.

BOILER The tank for heating water in a steam engine.

CRANKSHAFT A rod attached to a shaft and turned to run a machine.

DUAL INSTRUCTION Training with the instructor and student both in the plane.

ELEVATOR The moveable part of a tail plane which makes the airplane climb and dive.

LOW PRESSURE Faster moving air which can result in an airplane wing being sucked upward.

MONOPLANE An aircraft that has one set of wings.

OBSERVATION The act of watching enemy movements during war.

ORNITHOPTER An aircraft that has flapping wings.

PENDULUM A hanging weight that swings back and forth.

REVOLUTIONARIES People who fight for change.

RUDDER A hinged piece on the tail that is used to help steer the aircraft.

RUSSIAN REVOLUTION A series of revolutions in Russia in 1917 that led to the end of Czarist rule and the establishment of the Soviet government.

STREAMLINE A sleek design that allows an aircraft to pass easily through air.

STRUTS Rods used as support.

TAIL PLANE The wing on the back of a plane.

TETHERED Tied by a rope.

TRIPLANE An aircraft that has three sets of wings.